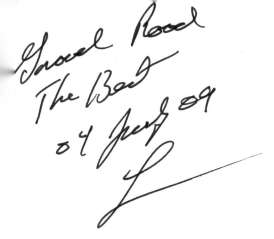

Gravel Road
The Best
04 July 09

Cork Tales

Wine Stories from Emperors to Pipsqueaks

Lance Greenwald

Warning: If You Buy This Book You are Part of a
Quest to Retell

Published in Nashville, Tennessee, by Lance Greenwald.
Typography by Publication Services, Inc., Champaign, Illinois.
ISBN: 0-9772075-0-1

Printed in the United States of America

Acknowledgements

We all wait with some apprehension as the Oscar recipient takes the microphone and starts a long list of "thank you's." This won't be so bad, I promise.

My father introduced me to French wines at twelve years of age. Each summer we would spend several weeks in León, where I learned a few of the stories you are about to read. I commenced upon this trip every year until I was sixteen. Then I discovered girls, and I had a different calling for a few years. Thanks, Pop.

Acknowledgements

Dana

My old wine bar partner who first coined the phrase "cork tale." It is easy for me to remember this because we stayed up late in those days and rarely spoke in complete sentences. Most conversations, emotions, challenges, and greetings were communicated by the word "dude."

Darlene

My confidant and companion who has brought sunrise to the sunset of my years.

Renee

My loyal colleague who translated my writings and wine-laden guttural utterings that at times were so unintelligible she had to ask the bartender to turn off the music.

Fred Platt, U.S.A.F. RETIRED

For a lifetime of stories and honor.

Acknowledgements

Duke Locicero at Café Giovanni
M. Atlas at Café Provence
Johnny Earles at Criolla's
Tim Creehan at Beach Walk Café
Archie Casbarian at Arnauds
Leann DeBeauchamp at Blue Buda Sushi Bar
Chris & Joyce at La Provance
Michele at Criolla's
The Sales Team & Jim Bozek at the
National Distributing Company

THE DASHING AND DEBONAIR LADIES AND
GENTLEMEN AT SEAGER'S RESTAURANT

Allen Davis of Davis Imports
Ed Moreau & the Ashers at M&J Imports
All of my friends and supporters in the
International Wine & Food Society

For sharing their food and wine knowledge over many years . . .

Dedication

This book is dedicated to Taylor and Carson—my past, my present, and my future—and to my "Comrades in Arms" who gave up their future, so that we may enjoy ours.

Introduction

Cork Tales is a storyteller's view of wine and of, in some cases, the people who lived on the land and affected world history. This is where fact meets fiction, where the myths of yesterday turn into the stories of today. The tales in this book are exactly that—a blend of history and fable. I now pass these on to you, the tales of the Cork.

After you read *Cork Tales*, you will be entrusted with their re-telling in the future. Just like the living softness that pours from wine bottles, new stories are being lived every day. Collect them as you would collect your memories.

Many of these stories are accompanied by Tasting Notes, bits of information which are indexed at the back of this book to cover everything from explaining additional facts to sharing Napoleon's own recipes.

The Tales

The Tales

Champagne

Veuve Clicquot

Champagne
Veuve Clicquot

There are three things you must remember about Champagne.

1. The vines are all around Epergne.
2. Champagne is marketed in Epergne and Reims.
3. The French will tell you that Champagne is not made anywhere else.

The spread of Champagne around the world was originally credited to the Emperor Napoleon and Napoleon

Bonaparte. When the French army would start a military campaign, one of their first stops was at the chalk caves of the Champagne Region of Reims. The soldiers then carried the Champagne far and wide.

Napoleon Bonaparte won many battles. At one point, he was engaged at Marengo, Italy. The evening prior to the battle, Napoleon's chef was planning dinner when he realized that he did not have the ingredients for Napoleon's favorite chicken dish, Chicken Veronique. The spices and local foods available above the town of Marengo, which were black olives and artichoke hearts, would have to do.

As the tale is told, Napoleon continued on in his campaign. Upon hearing of his difficulties with a Naval blockade, Madame Clicquot, one of his favorite Champagne house owners, set out to bring Napoleon and his army Champagne. She succeeded in her adventure.

4

When Madame Clicquot's husband passed away, she stayed in control instead of allowing the family business to be taken over by another male family member, quite an unusual feat for a woman of her day. Since the word "widow" translates to "veuve," the champagne came to be known as Champagne Veuve Clicquot. The Widow Clicquot was later invested as a Grande Dame of France.

Like the vines they are written about, all of these stories take different turns but her family name is still one of the best Champagne houses in the world to this day. One of the most popular Champagnes shipped to the American market is the Veuve Clicquot, non-vintage gold label. The best of the line is Grande Dame, which is equal in taste to any top shelf Champagne. Under the foil of

Grande Dame, the cork has a picture of the Widow Clicquot and the bottle bears a sea anchor in tribute to her valor.

See Tasting Notes: A Little Story of Bogart

The Great Merchant

&

Shipping Company

"Barton & Guestier"

The Great Merchant
&
Shipping Company

"Barton & Guestier"

Barton & Guestier, the great merchant and shipping company, was established in 1739 by an Irishman named Abraham Barton. Thirty years later, the company was co-owned by the French family Guestier.

The wine handled by the French company became a favorite of a very prominent American general by the name of George Washington. In 1775, Barton & Guestier therefore endeavored to fulfill its commitment of shipping wine and goods to the American colonies. For this purpose, Daniel Guestier engaged the great French ship, La Grand Nancy. They loaded it down with French wines and supplies and set off for the colonies.

Upon reaching the colonial coast, the ship was met by a British blockade. Undaunted, and with flags flying, they forced their way through the blockade. The wine and supplies delivered by Barton & Guestier to General Washington helped the American cause for independence. General Washington later sullied his reputation by becoming a politician…just kidding.

Chateau Latour

Chateau Latour

The tower so prominently displayed on the label of Chateau Latour, although constructed in 1626, was not the first on what was to become the Chateau grounds. Built early in the 14th century, the first tower was a more fort-like structure located at the southern end of the Giroade Estuary. The structure protected the entrance of the river and the area from pirates. As you can see, the area of Chateau Latour has a long and golden history, but this is a story of gold, a Cork Tale of real gold, that is told today.

The story begins with the German occupation of France during World War II. As the German army advanced on Paris, the French government had to decide where to hide the gold bars of the National Treasury. Our tale is of the gold traveling by truck from Paris to Chateau Latour, where the gold was buried in the fields among the grapes.

For years, Latour was called the "Golden Chateau." Were they referring to the gold in the bottle or the gold in the ground?

See Tasting Notes: Latour

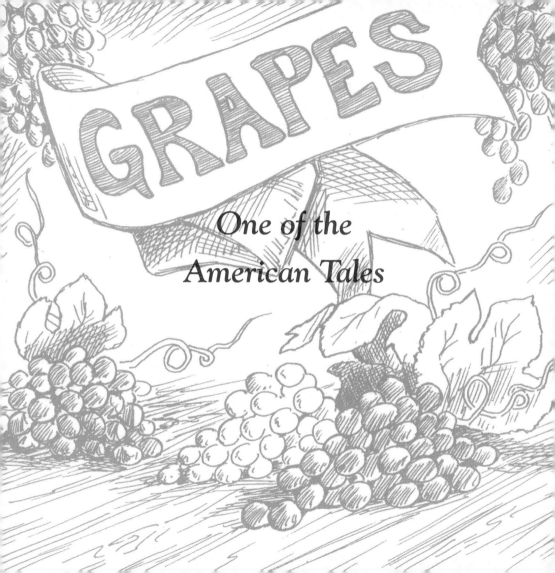

GRAPES

One of the

American Tales

One of the American Tales

I know you are all anticipating another tale about Mondavi, which is probably the most documented wine family of the new world. We may end up there, but the American wine story started long before California.

The story of American wine really starts at the end of the American Revolutionary War, or as we say in America, the "War of Foreign Aggression." The Longworth family of New Jersey remained faithful to the British Crown and lost everything at the end of the war. Nicholas Longworth, like many other Royalists, was forced to relocate. In the 1800's, he settled in the then little known frontier town of Cincinnati. For the next 50 years, he pursued real estate investments and became one of the wealthiest men in the area.

Longworth planted vineyards on some of his lands, and his wines were successful for many years. There were other efforts to produce excellent wine in the United States, but none had the success of the Longworth vineyards in southern Ohio, especially in the 1850's when his wines scored high marks as far away as Europe. Alas, however, his success ended quickly when his vines contracted a disease which stunted or killed growth during the next two decades.

The Longworth vineyards were one of the first successfully recorded wine producers in the continental United States. There were unsuccessful transplanting of

European vines as early as 1600, but most of these plants died. The first successful imported vines were from South Africa, which later came down to Nicholas Longworth and were the basis of his success in Cincinnati.

Longworth's most popular product was a sparkling wine produced in the traditional Champagne method. His sparkling Champagne wines were sold nationwide, which at that time extended to the Mississippi River, and in those days was still quite an achievement.

Most grapes grown in America in 1870 were sold as table fruit. The Concorde grape made wine with limited success. Another Concorde product became one of the still famous brands of our time. These grapes were used for an unfermented non-alcoholic juice, cultivated by Thomas Welch. The process was based on the same principals used by Louie Pasteur's pasteurization, a process which stopped yeast growth and fermentation.

Although California produced wines in the 1870's from many farms, the majority of California wines were made through the CWA or California Wine Association. By 1900, California was producing more wines than all of the Eastern states combined.

Now here's the point, dear Cork Tale reader, to this very sketchy and boring tale. Both Longworth and Welch were producing non-alcoholic products. They were both very conscious religious men of their time and part of America's growing abolition movement. They were both intent on making beverages that had less alcohol content, or in the case of Welch, no alcohol.

See Tasting Notes: One of the American Stories

Nelson's Blood
"Truly Barrel Aged"

Nelson's Blood
"Truly Barrel Aged"

The British fleet under Vice-Admiral Horatio Nelson lay to sea thirty miles, on the twentieth of October, 1805. As the British tell the story, the French fleet that had taken refuge in Cadiz, not having knowledge that the British fleet was in the area, sailed out of port.

Fleets of that day communicated by sending smaller ships' frigates' to the horizon. These ships communicated with Nelson's main fleet, which remained out of sight until the French and Spanish fleets were at sea and could not return to their ports. Sailing a parallel course twenty miles to the west, Nelson waited for the right moment. At 4:00 a.m., he turned the British fleet to engage the French and Spanish fleets southwest of Trafalgar.

Though heavily outnumbered, Nelson's battle plan was to sail two in lines abreast, letting the French and Spanish fleets "cross the T" of his flagship, Victoria. He knew that when the enemy came in range, he would take the first broadside but then tacking, he would bring his fleet against the last half of the French and Spanish battle line. This tactic had proved successful throughout his naval career.

The battle was ultimately fought at close quarters, and was eventually won by the British forces, which sank or captured eighteen ships of the enemy's line. However, the British leader did not fare so well. As the ships closed for battle, Nelson's physician, among others, reminded him that while standing on the quarter deck, resplendent in his admiral's uniform, he made a perfect target for snipers hidden in the enemy ship's upper rigging. Well into the battle, Nelson was shot by a sniper. Covering his face with a scarf so that his shipmates would not see him wounded, Nelson was taken below where he subsequently died of his wounds.

To preserve his remains, the body was placed in a keg of Royal Navy Rum. As the Victoria (Nelson's flagship) made its way back to England, the sailors and officers drank the Rum from the keg, along with Nelson's blood.

The custom of the British Navy at the time was to give portions of rum to the sailors each day. The officer in charge of the Rum was the purser, the paymaster. Over the years and drinks, purser became slurred into "pusser." Purser Rum still makes "Nelson's Blood" today. The Admiral's battle cry was "every man must do his duty to god and the crown." Do your duty, Cork Talers, and have a drink of Nelson's Blood…arrgh!

See Tasting Notes: Purser's Rum

A Trilogy of
Fog Cork Tales

A Trilogy of
Fog Cork Tales

The evening fog has played an intriguing role in the next three Cork Tales, the Trilogy of Fog Cork Tales.

The first tale is called Ghost Gum. In the hills and valleys of central Australia, there grow many vineyards and parcels. These particular vines are surrounded by an unusual type of eucalyptus tree. At a certain point of the year, as the evenings become cooler, the eucalyptus tree secretes a white sap that covers the entire tree. As the fog rolls in, these trees seem to float over the vineyards that they protect. Perhaps they are not protecting the vines, but are rather looking for a drink of the Ghost Gum Pinot or Chardonnay that BPE vineyard produces. Their bottle is distinguished by two eucalyptus leaves as its only adornment. The eucalyptus leaf has many uses, including fish poison, but there is no poison in these bottles, just everimproving wine.

The second Cork Tale of the Trilogy involves one of the most written about wine makers of our time, Robert Mondavi. As the story goes, Mondavi was looking over a consignment of Sauvignon Blanc when the morning fog inspired him to call the wine "Fume Blanc." This white smoke form of Sauvignon Blanc has been one of his most consistent sellers since its inception in 1966.

Lastly, let me tell you about Chateau d'Yquem, the most perfect wine of its kind in the world. It is blessed with a mist that has been known by many names throughout the years. The magic of its liquid bath on the grape is said to be the final touch before the harvest begins. During the harvest at night, the hillside is alive with pickers who each carry twinkling lights used to shine behind the grapes in order to inspect for the perfect color and maturity. The perfection of this wine is based on the exact moment when the sugar content is perfect, to begin the wine-making process of fermentation.

See Tasting Notes: Diamonds in the Mist

Isosceles

Isosceles

So you always wanted to say goodbye to the city, go to California and grow grapes, throw away your power neckties and the choking worry associated with them. You see yourself appearing in wine magazines with the sun setting through your now golden hair and a glass of your award winning Pinot in your hand, shot through with the sun's rays.

You bought the ground; in fact, you sold the deal so well, that the banker you told the story to fell in love with you and your idea, and is now your wife. She also appears in wine magazines now, rolling hills of grapevines frame her soft, subtle figure, clothed in what could only be called California wine country chic.

Now dear Cork Tale reader, before I tell you how they got that picture, and a top wine spectator rating, I want you to think about what you would do with that dream and that mountainside of dirt and rocks.

Going about their vineyard to be, they took core samples of the rocks and earth, and traveled to France. Those core samples were compared against the dirt of the French countryside in order to find the closest soils that grew the best vines of the Trilogy of wines that make up the Bordeaux blend. The results were outstanding. Purchased in 1981, their first crush was in 1987. In 1994, they won best blended red wine worldwide in the Pichon Longueville

Comtesse de LaLande. The *Wine Spectator* voted their 1997 Isosceles the sixth best wine in the world in 2000.

The leaves closest to the grape clusters are hand picked away to let the grapes ripen into full maturity. The Isosceles name comes from three sides of its namesake triangle. The smaller sides represent Merlot and Cabernet Franc, and the larger side, the majority of the blend, Cabernet Sauvignon.

To find out the vintner's name, dear Cork Tale reader, make reservations at the "Just Inn" and discover the perfect blend of success and charm.

La Chryma
de Christi

La Chryma de Christi

The vines of La Chryma de Christi, which have inspired many a tale, lay on the lower steps of Mount Vesuvius. One tale involves Lucifer, who was an archangel before he fell out of favor. Upon being cast from God's presence, he brought a piece of heaven, arriving on earth on his way to the lower levels. This part of heaven became the beautiful Gulf of Naples. When God realized what had happened, he wept and where his tears fell, the first wine vines grew on earth. These vines were later cultivated by man into La Chryma de Christi.

Another tale of these infamous vines concerns the eruption of Mount Vesuvius, which occurred on August 24 in the year 79 A.D. One of many eruptions, this massive disaster buried the Roman town of Pompeii. Years later when archeologists excavated the town, they found that time had stood still as the rivers of ash killed everything within its reach. The explorations of the perfectly preserved town revealed that the most popular businesses had been wine shops.

Heavenly tears over the destruction of Pompeii again led to the growth of vines, this time on Mount Vesuvius. These wines have come down to us as La Chryma de Christi, "The tears of Christ." Produced in both red and white, the wines are full-bodied and full of history. As you add to this journal, you will find many more Cork Tales from this region to re-tell as your own.

Too Much Sake

Too Much Sake

Ancient Japanese emperors kept a palace in the city of Nara, south of Tokyo, on the main island of Honshu. On these temple grounds lay a deer park. Many generations ago, as the Cork Tale turns, the Japanese crown prince was playing along the banks of the river that ran through the park. The prince's guardian, asleep from too much Sake, did not see the young child fall into the river. Shouts of danger awoke him in time to see a large buck deer drag the crown prince to safety.

Upon hearing the story, the Emperor pronounced the following royal decree. No male deer was to be harmed from that day forward; they would be forever protected by law. If a deer was found dead on a farmer's land, the farmer would be put to death. The first to go was the prince's Sake-soaked guardian.

From that time on for many centuries, each morning the Japanese farmer would rise before the sun to search his lands. If he found a dead deer on his land, he would drag it to his neighbor's property to avoid the death sentence. And that my trusting Cork Tale follower, is how passing the buck got started...no, really!

See Tasting Notes: Sake

The Cave That Never Was

The Cave That Never Was

The Sequoia Winery is a gorgeous landmark in the Napa Valley of California. One of its most distinguishing features is a giant Sequoia tree composed of two trees grown together.

The Sequoia vineyard, which lies very close to the Mondavi and Opus One vineyards, was established by a Midwesterner who migrated to California to become a grape grower. Having enjoyed an initial success at the business, he soon began to run out of storage. Possessing little engineering experience and less planning, he dug a tunnel-like cave to store his wine.

Some six years later, as the story goes, his neighbor, Robert Mondavi, inspected the storage structure and decided he would also build a storage cave. Unfortunately, his luck and skill in winemaking did not extend to cave digging. Well into the construction, he hit a hot spring that completely flooded the cave.

Marengo
"A Recipe for Victory"

Marengo

"A Recipe for Victory"

This Cork Tale starts at the end of the French Revolutionary Wars. The time was June 14, 1800, in northern Italy, and the place was around the town of Marengo. Our Cork Tale is really about chicken and Champagne, but first, the battle.

The Austrian army, led by Lt. General Melas, crossed the Bonmida River in northern Italy and attacked the French line. Believing that the main assault would come from a different area, First Consul Napoleon Bonaparte had dispatched part of his troop to two different locations. As the morning fighting continued, the Austrian army began making headway against Napoleon's reduced forces, and the French started an orderly withdrawal by mid-afternoon.

Napoleon, now convinced that this company was the main attacking force, recalled his two divisions of infantry. By the time General Boudet's division entered the battle along with General Kellenmann and 600 mounted heavy cavalry, the French army was in full retreat. With the addition of these forces, the French army counterattacked, causing the surrender of 2,000 Austrian soldiers at the front of the pursuit. The remaining Austrian army reformed and managed to hold the town of Marengo until evening. They then withdrew, and Napoleon won the battle.

There are many interpretations of the decisions made that day in 1800, and I invite you to investigate them. Our Cork Tale is really just a footnote to the battle. As evening fell, Napoleon's chef informed him that he could not find the ingredients for his favorite poultry dish, Chicken Veronique. None-the-less, the first Consul did dine on chicken that night. However, his dish was cooked with local ingredients including tomatoes, olives, red wine, and pasta. This recipe, passed down to us through the years, is known as Chicken Marengo. If I do say so myself, one of the finest presentations can be enjoyed at Café Provence in Destin, Florida.

Cork Tales

The drink, as always, was Champagne. As the French say, there are only two times in life to drink Champagne— "in defeat because you need it, and in victory because you deserve it." June 14, 1800 was a day for both!

See Tasting Notes for Recipes: Chicken Marengo & Chicken Veronique

The Greatest
Wine Taster of All

The Greatest
Wine Taster of All

In 1855, at the time of the Paris Exposition, the French categorized their wines into growths. Wines were classified as to their taste and growth in the Chateau's specific boundaries. Additions to these lands by the Chateaus caused long opposition to their classification with the original Chateau. An example of these is Chateau Mouton & Chateau Le Forte Latour. However, little is written about the categorizing and tasting of wine prior to 1855 and that is where this Cork Tale begins—in the 1300's.

In 1301, Philip Le Bel defined the profession of wine magistrate. The wine magistrate's function was to maintain the quality of wines in Bordeaux and Burgundy. The magistrate would go to the Chateau storage, the Chai. He would use a hammer with a screw punch (a piqueurs) to punch a hole in the barrel and taste the wine to see if it met the proper standards. Not only was he the *Wine Spectator* and Parker rating of his day, the wine magistrate had legal authority to prevent the sale of the wine if it failed to meet his approval. The wine would be spilled, or poured out, instead. His title was La Courtier (Broker) Piqueur (punching).

One of the most famous Cork Tales occurred in 1804 in the Medoc at Chateau Lis Trac. The Courtier, Hubert Bontemps, tasted from a 500 bottle keg of wine. Summarizing that the wine had hints of metal and rope, with an aftertaste of cardboard, he refused to release it for sale! After the barrel was drained of its 500 bottles, there was found in the bottom of the barrel a key to the cellar with a rope holding the cardboard identifying tag. One key! One piece of hemp! And one piece of cardboard in the bottom of 500 fifths of wine! That, mon amie, is a great-tasting Cork Tale!

The Pope's Wine

The Pope's Wine

In 1305, the Bishop of Bordeaux was elected the first French Pope. Upon his selection, the bishop took up residence at the Chateauneuf in Avignon, which is seven miles from the edge of Avignon. Pope Clement V was the first of seven popes that resided in Avignon, "the new home of the Pope."

A total of six French popes followed Clement V, and there was always a conflict between the Roman Church and the French heritage of these papal rulers. Storytellers and historians have filled volumes of books of the "Great

Schism," the controversial breach of the Catholic church of France from Rome.

The work on the Chateau and the resulting control of the vineyards, won over the local farmer's commitment to his local eminence. This was an unusual time because there were always allegiance changes in all levels of European society, and the church was usually involved. Now for many generations, the head of the Catholic Church was no longer in Rome, but in Avignon—according to the French.

Pope Clement V, after creating his own papacy at Avignon in France, split from the Vatican. The wine produced at the Chateau was called "Chateauneuf-du-Pape." There were many producers, mostly Red Rhone wine. The color of the wine is brown and red, but they also do produce excellent white wines, full and rich, also called Chateauneuf-du-Pape.

One wall of the original Chateau still remains high on a hill with vineyards stretching to the horizon in all directions. These vines are planted in very rocky soil made up of a covering of rounded stones that retain the day's heat, which helps ripen the grapes and provides excellent drainage. These vineyards are prime examples of the "Struggling Vine Theory," which suggests that wines made from the grapes of vines planted in the rugged hillsides, literally struggling for existence, are the best wines.

Although the wine makers are allowed to use thirteen different grapes, the two primary grapes that produce the Pope's wine are Grenache (pronounced Greh-NAHSH), and Syrah (pronounced See-RAH). These wines keep very well over the years, and their high tannins fade into beautiful mellow wines, excellent with game birds and lighter meats.

Although made by many producers in Burgundy, Chateauneuf-du-Pape still bears the papal crest on the bottle. Most are reds, but there is a production of white, full-bodied Chateauneuf. All worth the tasting.

See Tasting Notes: The Pope's Wine

A Port Tale

Platt
Port
1941

A Port Tale

Sir Burden, dressed in the fashion of the day, was obviously a gentleman. So why was he watching the unloading of a British tradesman ship on the London docks, instead of being at home with his ravishing red-headed wife? It does not really matter what year it was because this Cork Tale covers a tradition that dates back to the seventeenth century.

When the British first tried Portuguese wine, they found it sweet and light as compared to the French Claret of which they were so fond. Port today is a fortified wine composed of 4/5 wine, and 1/5 Brandy, which raises the alcohol content to 18 percent, as compared to the 11-12 percent alcohol content of unfortified wine. But back to Sir Burden.

The gentleman was honoring an age old tradition, having recently become a new father. He was waiting at the docks, like his father before him, to acquire a case of new Port. Hopefully, it would be a vintage year in the "Duro." In Portugal, not all wine years are declared as vintage years. When a vintage year is declared, there is a certain amount of gamesmanship as the smaller producers watch the larger houses—Sanderman, Grahams, Offiely—to see if they would declare a vintage year. If you are wondering why these names are British instead of Portuguese, it is because British interests have controlled most of the larger Port distributors for many years.

Sir Burden was in luck. He bought a wooden case of the new Port and took it home to his family. The Port was presented at his son Grant's birthday, as it would be at succeeding birthdays. The family would write the events of the day on the case, but it would not be opened until the child's twenty-first birthday. On that date, the father would open the case of Port and share that special conversation that all fathers dread, questions to which all sons already know the answers anyway. Then with his glass of Port, Grant Burden would become a man. The remainder of the case would be given to him to enjoy during future memorable events in his life.

If you review the history of Port, you will see that in 1756 the demand for Port had outpaced the production.

This was a highly unregulated industry at the time. The producers were pushed to the point of adding elderberry juice to the Port cuvee. The practice became so widespread, that the governing body eventually ordered all of the Mulberry trees in the growing regions cut down! The Marquis De Pombal was commissioned to strengthen the controls of the industry. He established The Old Wine Company, which over the years stabilized the price and quality of Port wine.

At the beginning of the fermentation process, Brandy is introduced to the cuvee—one part Brandy for every four parts wine. The introduction of Brandy stops the fermentation process instantly, and the sweet, heavy, red Port wines are left in bottles to age to their full maturity.

I have traveled the Duro River and visited the city of Porto at its end. The Duro River is 560 miles long and has changed little in the 200 years of reported Port history. Through great personal sacrificing, I have tasted the listed Port wines below, and I offer them to you as a tasting guide.

1997	Outstanding/ Hold
1995	Outstanding/ Hold
1994	Classic/ Hold
1992	Classic/ Hold
1991	Classic/ Hold
1987	Very good
1986	Good
1984	Drink
1978–83	Drink
1972–76	Drink

There are many more Port Cork Tales you can discover on your own, as I am into my third Port boot and falling asleep. I will leave them to our next book, Son of Cork Tales.

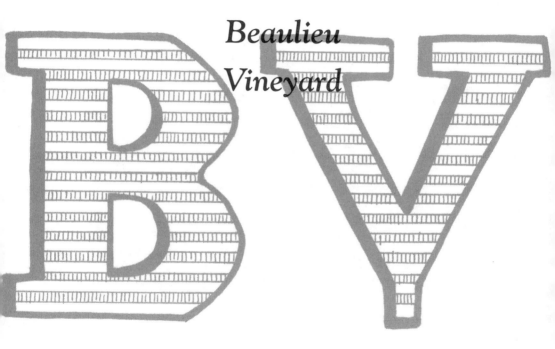

Beaulieu
Vineyard

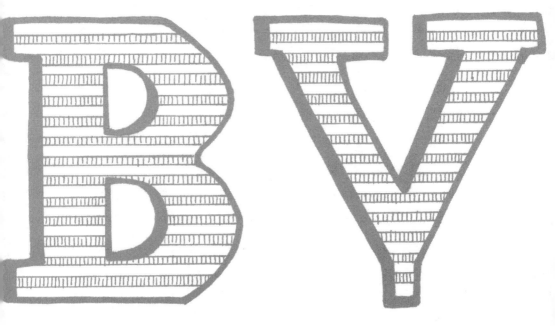

Beaulieu Vineyard

Beaulieu Vineyard was founded in 1900 by George de Lator. The wines produced here have been some of the best produced in Napa Valley.

B.V. was one of the first California vineyards to use the term "private reserve" on their George Lator Cabernet. If they were not the first to use the term, their George Lator Cabernet wine is certainly the first in taste.

Of all the wine and liquor producers in the United States that went through prohibition, B.V. was one of the few who legally did not stop production, as they were chosen by the Catholic Church to produce sacramental wines.

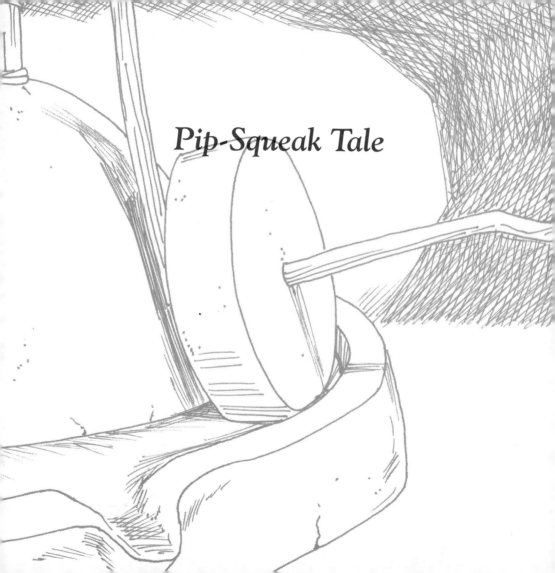

Pip-Squeak Tale

Pip-Squeak Tale

In the 1800's, a great deal of American wine was produced by rolling a large stone over the grapes. The juice would then run into a vat. The idea was to crush the grapes without crushing the seeds within. If the seeds were broken, the cuvee would take on a bitter taste. The winemaker would listen carefully as he crushed the grapes, not wanting to hear the pip-squeak of a broken seed.

Chateau Beychevelle
"Another Admiral's Tale"

Chateau Beychevelle
"Another Admiral's Tale"

If a person's eyes are truly windows to their souls, some wine labels are windows to the history and soul of the living liquid inside the bottle they adorn. Chateau Beychevelle has such a label, one that depicts an old sailing ship, and that is where our Cork Tale begins.

If you were sitting on the banks of the Gironde River, on the Isle Bouchard across from the Chateau, you would notice all the wine ships and barges that lower their sails to half mast as they pass Beychevelle. As the French ships pass the Chateau, they lower their sails to half mast to honor Admiral Beychevelle, one of the original owners.

The admiral title was awarded to Beychevelle by King Henri III, as one story goes, but there are many variations to this Cork Tale, since many French-titled families have owned the property over the centuries. Some say that the lowered sail is a translation of the French "beche velle." I prefer to think of an admiral in full military dress standing beneath a grand cedar tree, "Cedar of Lebanon," on the Chateau's grounds, receiving the lowered sail honors of the ships that pass on the river.

If you notice the head mast of the ship, you will see a Griffin. The Griffin was the guardian of Dionysus, the

Greek god of wine, and it guards the prow of the Bey-chevelle ship.

The vineyard produces a fourth growth Bordeaux, sold as Chateau Beychevelle, and a second wine that is sold under the title of Admiral Beychevelle. The wine is like pouring rubies from a bottle and is one of my favorites.

I invite you, dear Cork Tale reader, to research this Chateau, for like the ship on the bottle, the Cork Tale sails in many directions.

See Tasting Notes: Chateau Beychevelle

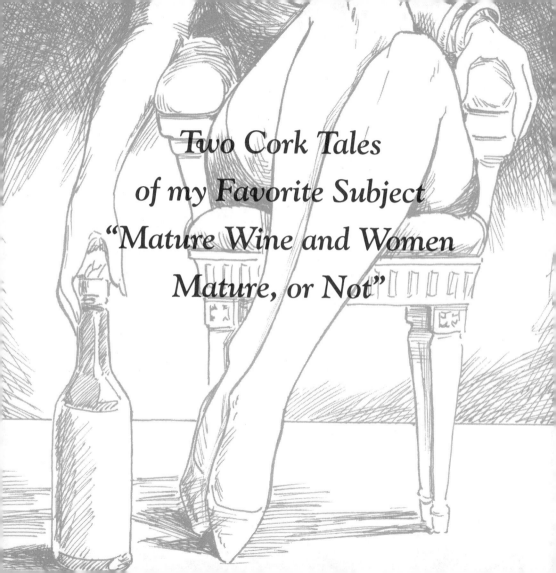

Two Cork Tales
of my Favorite Subject
"Mature Wine and Women
Mature, or Not"

Two Cork Tales
my Favorite Subject
"Mature Wine and Women
Mature, or Not"

Recently, the Royal London University College conducted a survey, headed by Sir Michael Marmot, over a six-year span. The study compared those who consumed at least two glasses of wine a week to those who did not consume wine at all. The survey was taken by 6,000 government employees. My personal idea of hell would be to have to confront 6,000 British government employees who did not drink for six years.

The Chef at Café Provence in Destin, who told me this Cork Tale, wanted it clearly understood that the French had nothing to do with the study. The results, which were quite conclusive, showed that the group who drank the wine had a much higher retention rate, and that the wine stimulated their brain. When the results were broken down by gender, the women performed even better than the men. The results of this study were published in Royal London's University, April 10–21, 2004 edition.

Women, smarter than men. I knew that; no, really!

Our second Cork Tale in this chapter concerns two young women who, having recently completed a wine tour of Europe, sat in contemplation of their future in a delightful Paris café. As their travels as singles drew to an end, the women's thoughts turned to mates. Having just taken in all of Europe's wine countries, they decided to classify the best and worst characteristics that they had found in men.

The perfect man, they decided, should cook like a Frenchman, possess the qualities of a German engineer, practice the patience of a British policeman, have the organization of the Swiss, and make love like an Italian (with a much longer span of attention than most Italian lovers...just kidding).

After consuming another bottle of wine, they decided the worst combination would be a British cook who was a German policeman or a French engineer who made love like the Swiss and organized his life like an Italian.

Both women lived very full lives and are experts in wine and divorce.

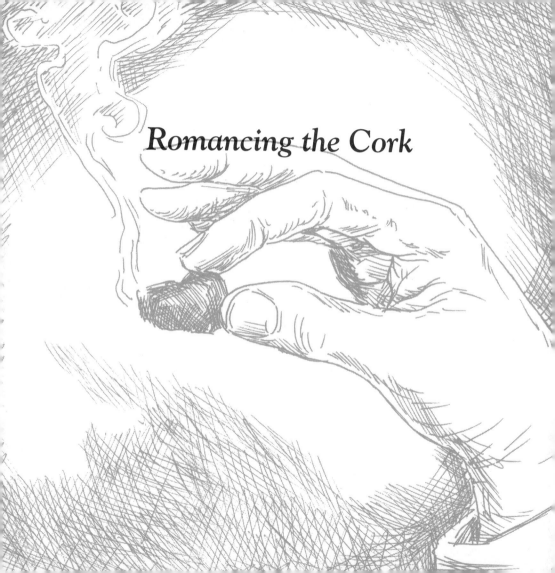

Romancing the Cork

Romancing the Cork

Now what would a book entitled Cork Tales be without a story about the Cork itself? Let me formally introduce you, my dear Cork Tale adventurer, to Mr. Quercus Suber, or as his friends call him, the Cork Tree. To communicate with him, you should use your best Spanish or Portuguese. No. . . . I said your best Spanish or Portuguese, not Dos Tequila, por favor.

The Cork Tree existed side by side with wine makers for many centuries without them ever coming together. Prior to the twelfth century, wine was never aged but was consumed prior to its spoiling. Later the glass blowers near

Venice, still very much in existence today, first began producing glass bottles with small necks that made air tight storage with corks possible. Of course, corks beget corkscrews. The first was a modified gun worm, the tool used to clean or retrieve a stuck bullet from a musket, a bullet screw. Enough history dear Cork Tale reader, now for the romance.

To become a romantic with your cork, you must abide precisely by the following instructions. She has accepted your invitation to dinner with the promise of an exciting experience. She looks beautiful over the table's candlelight. You have browsed the wine list, selected Chambertan for your first wine of the evening, pronounced it correctly, and now the aloof wine steward is presenting you with the cork.

Ignore him. Keep talking to your date, remembering that if you screw this up the outside of her beautiful dress is all you will ever see of her. Casually pick up the cork, feeling the bottom for dampness across its entire surface, touch her hand as you raise the cork to your nose, inhaling briefly, and toss the cork on the table, barely nodding to the wine steward.

Later in the evening, after the red wine and the Port, take the cork, hold it in the table's candle flame, turning it to produce a charred end. Then with a grand gesture, use the cork to sketch a likeness of her on the table cloth or linen napkin, depending on which one you want the restaurant to add to your dinner bill. Done correctly, she will fall into your arms, saving the cork for her own personal Cork Tale, and be yours for life . . . or maybe a shorter period.

See Tasting Notes: The Cork

Losing Your
Fear of Wine

Losing Your
Fear of Wine

Learning about wine and expressing yourself is easy. It just has to be done one bottle at a time! Don't worry about not being able to taste the pear overtones and the pencil shaving finish. Clear your palate, take a sip, then inhale and see how your mouth reacts to the wine. If it is bitter to the taste, try another. Just like the perfect mate, the perfect wine is out there waiting for you.

When you find a wine that you like, buy three or more bottles, check your wine encyclopedia or your computer, open the wine, and while you're drinking it, read both sides of the label and look up the wine in your information sources.

Don't be disappointed if you don't find the exact label. As you become more familiar with the wine growing regions, the information on the label will bring you to a close approximation of your wine's birth and bottling. Wine labels will tell you the country of origin, the region in the country of origin, the domain (an area that encompasses wine growing areas), and the Chateau, or vineyard for Chateau bottled wine. Chateau bottled wine usually means that the grapes used to make the wine were grown at the Chateau.

After you have researched your wine and tasted it, the next step is to share the second bottle with friends, so that you can repeat what you have just learned. You will then become an expert, one bottle at a time!

Your Tales to Retell

Your Tales to Retell

Well, I have to get my tale, cork or otherwise, out of here. We've gone from emperors to admirals, and from popes to pip-squeaks. I hope you've enjoyed reading these Cork Tales as much as I have enjoyed putting them together. Now you are armed with Cork Tales from the distant past, some still shrouded in the midst of prerecorded history. I give them to you in an age where computers can process information at septillion operations per second (that's a 1 followed by 42 zeros).

Cork Tales

The wine in front of you is a living thing. It will be different tomorrow. The grapes were hand picked and nurtured for years by a grape farmer who's not interested in today's speed, but yesterday's quality.

Retell one the next time you're watching a sunset, and drink a glass of Rose Champagne. There's a certain time in every sunset that the colors of the Champagne and the rays of the setting sun, match for a brief moment. The sky and the glass become one. That's when you say "You know, I heard a wine story the other day, a Cork Tale."

Tasting Notes

Veuve Clicquot—"Casablanca"

Veuve Clicquot is ordered for Major Strasser by Captain Renault, the Veuve Clicquot 26. The famous toast "Here's looking at you kid," was Corton Rouge, still made today and manufactured as Mumm's Corton Rouge, and has a stripe across the label, as in the movie.

Romancing the Cork

A cork tree has to grow for 25 years before it can be stripped for its bark. But to obtain cork quality, the tree must be 50 years old. The cork obtained after being treated, produces an average wine cork of 800 million cells with elasticity, which produces the perfect bottle seal.

Sake

Although Sake is called rice wine, the process to produce it is closer to the way beer is made, rather than the fermentation process to wine making. The hangover, however, is more like the process of dying.

Chateauneuf-du-Pape

The raised mark on the glass bottle's neck was originally produced under Roman (some say Greek) rule. The mark was placed on the bottle so merchants would fill your flask to that level, thereby ensuring that you would receive a full measure of wine. The raised glass on today's modern Chateauneuf-du-Pape is the papal symbol.

One of the American Stories

European vines brought to America soon died from Phylloxera, a microscopic insect that attaches to the vine's roots. By the time the wine grower sees his vine dying, the insect has already killed that vine and has moved on to a healthier one, making discovery difficult. American vines had developed immunity to Phylloxera, and the resulting grafting of American vine roots to European vines stopped the plague.

When Phylloxera started affecting European vines, they delayed grafting American roots to the vines, believing that it would affect the end product's taste, the wine. In the late 1880's, with no other place to turn, American rootstocks were grafted to the vines of Burgundy and the vines were saved. Americans will tell you that all French

vines were grown from American vines. As you can see, this was not the case. Phylloxera came from America and the disease resistant American rootstock stopped it from spreading.

Fermentation in grape skins determines wine's color. Wine is 86% water, and 11–12% alcohol (ethyl alcohol). The 3–4% remaining components are called Phenolic and Tannins, which account for the wine's color and flavor.

Social movements, dear Cork Tale reader, resulted in a devastating event to the American wine industry on December 17, 1917—the 19th Amendment to the Constitution of the United States and the Age of Prohibition. What's wrong with a country that takes a grape and makes a non-alcoholic Welch's product that has more success than most vineyards? I tell you, mon amie, this would not

happen in France—so many grapes and no wine! Sacre bleu!

Nelson's Blood

Purser's Rum is produced in the Caribbean, Trinidad, the BVI, and Guyana. It is dark and 95.5% proof. The next time you visit St. Johns, drink a shot of "Nelson's Blood" at the Purser's Rum store and Grog Bar to the right of the ferry landing. Grog is a mixture of rum, sugar, lime juice, and water. The British Navy policy of the Purser giving out daily shots of Rum ended in 1870.

Chateau Latour

The making of Chateau Latour is a little different from the other Bordeaux blends. All Bordeaux blends have

Cabernet Sauvignon and Merlots as their base, with a much smaller percentage of Cabernet Franc. Latour adds another varietal, Petit Verdot. LaForte Latour is the second label of Latour and is produced on a revitalized acreage of the estate.

Chateau d'Yquem, Diamonds in the Mist

In the southern part of Bordeaux, there lies an unusual vineyard. Since its establishment in 1593, the Chateau d'Yquem has produced the top wine of its class. The Chateau is approximately 457 acres, planted mostly with Semillon grapes. The grapes are left to mature well into the fall of the year. Each evening they are covered with a mist that is associated with a noble rot (Botrytis Cinerea). This reduces the water content inside each of the grapes

and raises the natural sugar level. The harvest can go on for some time, by picking each grape by hand at the precise moment of ripeness. As evening falls, lights are used by the pickers to look through each grape to determine its level of perfection. The process is so exacting that it is estimated that one bunch of grapes ends up producing only a single glass of wine. Looking up into the hills in the evening, the twinkling lights of the harvesters are diamonds in the sky, producing a "gem of wine."

Chateau Beychevelle

Chateau Beychevelle's bottle is filled with a fourth growth Bordeaux.

Recipe for Chicken Veronique

> 1 (3-lb.) fryer, cut into pieces
> 1/2 lemon
> 1/3 cup butter
> 1 garlic clove, minced
> 1/3 cup Sauterne
> 1 cup seedless grapes
> pinch of paprika
> lemons

Rub chicken with lemon and let sit for 15 minutes. Brown chicken in butter for about 10 minutes. Add garlic and sauté for 30 seconds. Add Sauterne. Simmer for 25 minutes or until chicken is just tender. Add grapes and heat through. Serve over noodles. Garnish with paprika and decoratively cut lemons. Selected wine: Chardonnay

Recipe for Chicken Marengo

> 1/2 chicken (cut up)
> 1/2 cup chopped mushrooms
> 1/4 cup chopped Spanish onions
> 1/2 cup black olives
> 1/2 cup artichoke hearts
> 1/2 cup red wine
> 1/2 cup white wine
> 1/2 cup tomato sauce
> pinch of oregano
> pinch of salt
> pinch of pepper

Combine mushrooms, onions, black olives, artichoke hearts, and the other spices. Brown ingredients in olive oil. Add white and red wine, and tomato sauce. Bring to a boil, and then reduce heat. Brown chicken in olive oil. Cover with sauce. Place in oven for 30 minutes at 350°F.

About the Author

Lance lives in Destin, Florida, which he discovered in his Air Force years. His past writings (he wouldn't call them literary achievements) include financial articles, wine columns for newspapers, and wine magazine stories.

He's very interested in your Cork Tales. Would you be so kind enough to share them with him? He might want to include them in a future project. E-mail Lance at lance@corktales.com.

Your Tasting Notes

Your Tasting Notes

Your Tasting Notes

Your Tasting Notes